Subtraction

1−1=0	3−3=0	5−5=0	7−7=0	9−9=0
2−1=1	4−3=1	6−5=1	8−7=1	10−9=1
3−1=2	5−3=2	7−5=2	9−7=2	
4−1=3	6−3=3	8−5=3	10−7=3	10−10=0
5−1=4	7−3=4	9−5=4		
6−1=5	8−3=5	10−5=5	8−8=0	
7−1=6	9−3=6		9−8=1	
8−1=7	10−3=7	6−6=0	10−8=2	
9−1=8		7−6=1		
10−1=9	4−4=0	8−6=2		
	5−4=1	9−6=3		
2−2=0	6−4=2	10−6=4		
3−2=1	7−4=3			
4−2=2	8−4=4			
5−2=3	9−4=5			
6−2=4	10−4=6			
7−2=5				
8−2=6				
9−2=7				
10−2=8				

WORD PROBLEM—SOLVING FUN

YOU CAN, TOUCAN, MATH

BY DAVID A. ADLER · ILLUSTRATED BY EDWARD MILLER

Holiday House / New York

With each number riddle, first decide which operation—addition, subtraction, multiplication, or division—you will use to solve the riddle. Then solve it.

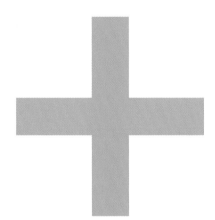

Add to find the total of two or more numbers.

Subtract to find the difference between two numbers.

Multiply to find the total of the same number added two or more times.

Divide to find how many times one number can go into another number.

TWO TOUCANS

Two toucans,
and seven,
and four toucans more—
how many toucans
are two, seven, and four?

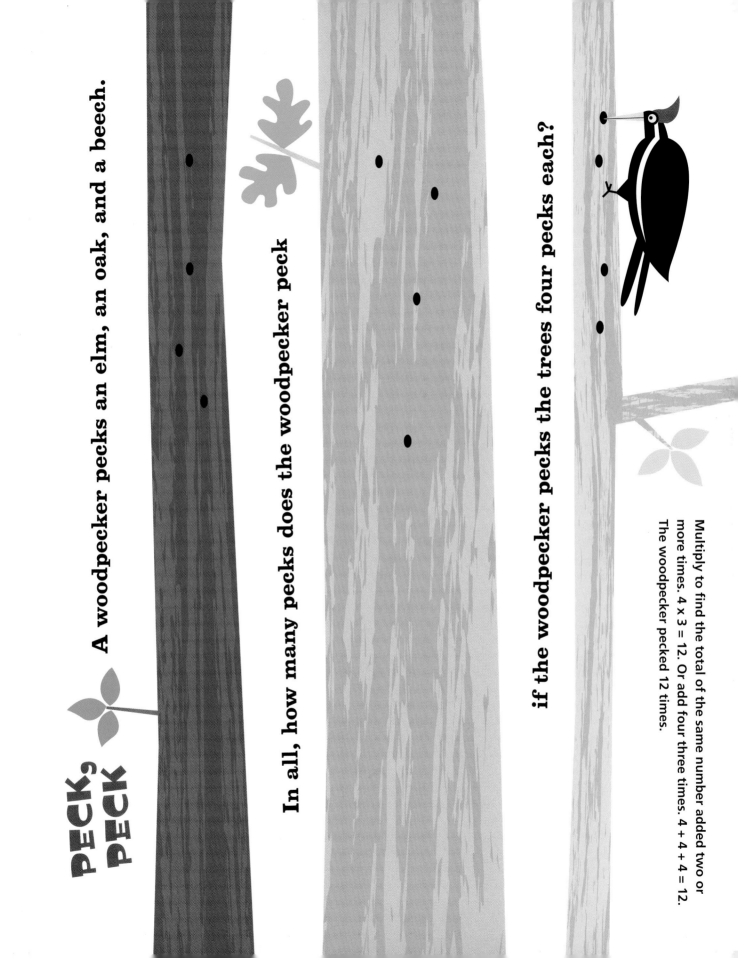

PECK, PECK

A woodpecker pecks an elm, an oak, and a beech.

In all, how many pecks does the woodpecker peck

if the woodpecker pecks the trees four pecks each?

Multiply to find the total of the same number added two or more times. 4 x 3 = 12. Or add four three times. 4 + 4 + 4 = 12. The woodpecker pecked 12 times.

LEGS, LEGS, LEGS!

Each flamingo has two legs,

legs thin as sticks.

How many flamingoes together

have twenty-six?

Divide to find how many times one number can go into another number. 26 ÷ 2 = 13. There are 13 flamingoes.

LUNCHTIME FOR PELICANS

Two pelicans fishing.
Each catches a bunch.
How many fish
in the pelicans' lunch
if one catches seven
and the other eleven?

**Mary Hen lays
twenty eggs in four days.
If each day she lays
the same number,
I wonder
how many eggs each day
does Mary Hen lay?**

Divide to find how many times one number can go into another number. 20 ÷ 4 = 5. Mary Hen laid 5 eggs each day.

BEGIN WITH TEN WRENS

A desert bird
is the cactus wren.
We begin with ten.
Four fly off.
How many then
remain from the ten?

Subtract to find the difference between two numbers. 10 − 4 = 6. 6 wrens remain.

BLUEBIRD, BLUEBIRD

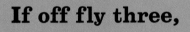

Seventeen bluebirds

in an evergreen tree.

If off fly three,

how many remain

in the evergreen tree?

Subtract to find the difference between
two numbers. 17 − 3 = 14. 14 bluebirds
remain in the evergreen tree.

QUIET, PLEASE!

**Robins resting
the first day of fall.
Six here.
Seven there.
How many in all?**

Add to find the total of two or more numbers.
6 + 7 = 13. There are 13 robins in all.

Multiply to find the total of the same number added two or more times. 7 x 6 = 42. Or add six seven times. 6 + 6 + 6 + 6 + 6 + 6 + 6 = 42. Or add seven six times. 7 + 7 + 7 + 7 + 7 + 7 = 42. The orioles would bring 42 bits of string.

NEST BUILDING

**Seven orioles
building nests in the spring.
If each oriole would bring
six bits of string,
how many bits in all
would the orioles bring?**

PLAIN PIPIT!
Twenty-four pipits all on a plain. Fourteen fly off. How many remain?

Subtract to find the difference between two numbers. 24 − 14 = 10. 10 pipits remain on the plain.

BY THE BAY

Twenty blue jays
by the bay.
Twelve fly off.
How many stay?

LOTS OF CHICKADEES

**Black-capped chickadees
perched in hickory trees.
Four hickories
each with six chickadees.
In all,
how many chickadees
in the hickories?**

GAR-OOO!
GAR-OOO!

Gar-ooo! Gar-ooo!
Hear the cranes call.
Four in the waters.
Five in the reeds.
Gar-ooo! Gar-ooo!
Hear the cranes call.
How many cranes
are there in all?

Add to find the total of two or more numbers.
4 + 5 = 9. There are 9 cranes in all.

LOONS AT THE LAKE

**Loons on the water
and under.
Twelve loons at the lake.
I wonder,
with seven up
how many under?**

Subtract to find the difference between two
numbers. 12 − 7 = 5. There are 5 loons under
the water.

THINK OF
THE BOBOLINK

**Now, please think
of the hungry bobolink.
The bobolink eats
nine grains of rice
and seven of wheat.
In all, how many grains
does the bobolink eat?**

Add to find the total of two or more numbers. 9 + 7 = 16. The bobolink eats 16 grains in all.

PEEP! PEEP!

A meadowlark
in the park
sitting on five eggs.
Peep! Peep!
Two hatch.
Now how many meadowlarks
in the park
still in the shell?

Subtract to find the difference between two numbers. 5 – 2 = 3. There are 3 meadowlarks still in the shell.

THREES IN TREES

Scissor-tailed flycatchers
sitting in trees.
Scissor-tailed flycatchers
sitting in threes.
Three to a tree.
Five trees in all.
How many scissor-tailed flycatchers
sitting in trees?

Multiply to find the total of the same number added two or more times. 3 x 5 = 15. Or add three five times. 3 + 3 + 3 + 3 + 3 = 15. Or add five three times. 5 + 5 + 5 = 15. There are 15 scissor-tailed flycatchers sitting in trees.

OBESE GEESE

**Twelve geese swimming
in a geese habitat.
Nine are thin,
the others fat.
How many obese geese
in the geese habitat?**

Subtract to find the difference between two numbers. 12 − 9 = 3. There are 3 obese geese.

JEEK! JEEK!

Listen to the cry
of the yellow-billed magpie.
Jeek! Jeek! Weg! Weg! Weg!
There are fourteen magpies,
but only eight
make the magpie cries.
How many magpies are quiet?

LOOK UP!

**A black-bellied plover
just flew over.
Here come two more,
now another four.
In all, how many plovers
flew over?**

CROWS IN ROWS

Thirty crows

in six rows,

with each row the same.

How many crows

in each of the rows?

For math teachers everywhere,
especially my brother Joe
—D. A. A.

The author thanks Professor Stephen Krulik of the Department
of Curriculum, Instruction, and Technology in Education of
Temple University for his help.

Text copyright © 2006 by David A. Adler
Illustrations copyright © 2006 by Edward Miller III

All Rights Reserved
Printed in the United States of America
www.holidayhouse.com
3 5 7 9 10 8 6 4 2

Library of Congress Cataloging-in-Publication Data

Adler, David A.
You can, toucan, math : word problem-solving fun / by David A. Adler ;
illustrated by Edward Miller.
p. cm.

ISBN-10: 0-8234-1919-3 (hardcover)
ISBN-13: 978-0-8234-1919-7 (hardcover)

1. Problem solving—Juvenile literature. 2. Word problems (Mathematics)—Juvenile literature.
I. Miller, Edward, 1964– ill. II. Title.

QA63.A33 2006
511.3'3—dc22
2005050339

ISBN-13: 978-0-8234-2117-6 (pbk)

The art for this book was created on the computer.
Book design by Edward Miller

Visit www.davidaadler.com for additional books by David A. Adler
Visit www.edmiller.com for additional books by Edward Miller

Multiplication

0x1=0	0x3=0	0x5=0	0x7=0	0x9=0
1x1=1	1x3=3	1x5=5	1x7=7	1x9=9
2x1=2	2x3=6	2x5=10	2x7=14	2x9=18
3x1=3	3x3=9	3x5=15	3x7=21	3x9=27
4x1=4	4x3=12	4x5=20	4x7=28	4x9=36
5x1=5	5x3=15	5x5=25	5x7=35	5x9=45
6x1=6	6x3=18	6x5=30	6x7=42	6x9=54
7x1=7	7x3=21	7x5=35	7x7=49	7x9=63
8x1=8	8x3=24	8x5=40	8x7=56	8x9=72
9x1=9	9x3=27	9x5=45	9x7=63	9x9=81
10x1=10	10x3=30	10x5=50	10x7=70	10x9=90

0x2=0	0x4=0	0x6=0	0x8=0	0x10=0
1x2=2	1x4=4	1x6=6	1x8=8	1x10=10
2x2=4	2x4=8	2x6=12	2x8=16	2x10=20
3x2=6	3x4=12	3x6=18	3x8=24	3x10=30
4x2=8	4x4=16	4x6=24	4x8=32	4x10=40
5x2=10	5x4=20	5x6=30	5x8=40	5x10=50
6x2=12	6x4=24	6x6=36	6x8=48	6x10=60
7x2=14	7x4=28	7x6=42	7x8=56	7x10=70
8x2=16	8x4=32	8x6=48	8x8=64	8x10=80
9x2=18	9x4=36	9x6=54	9x8=72	9x10=90
10x2=20	10x4=40	10x6=60	10x8=80	10x10=100